# The Rocky Shore

*Books by John M. Kingsbury*
SEAWEEDS OF CAPE COD AND THE ISLANDS
DEADLY HARVEST
POISONOUS PLANTS OF THE UNITED STATES AND CANADA

*Illustrated by Edward and Marcia Norman*
SEAWEEDS OF CAPE COD AND THE ISLANDS
A BEACHCOMBER'S BOTANY
THE SANDY SHORE
THE ATLANTIC SHORE
THE WINTER BEACH
BIRDS OF CAPE COD, MASSACHUSETTS

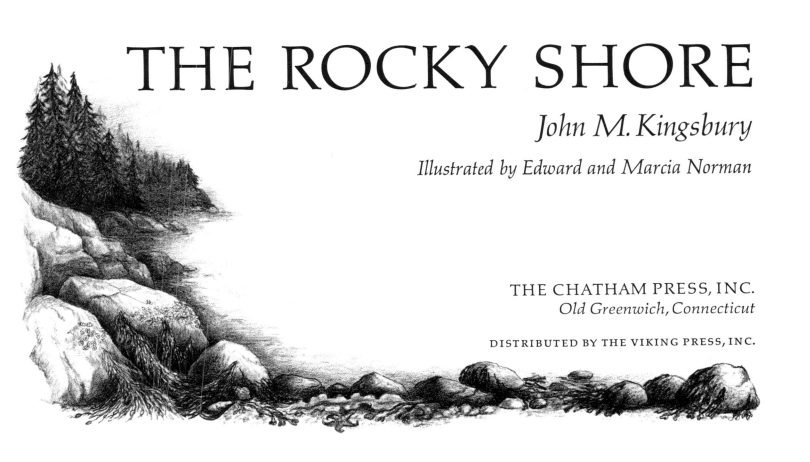

# THE ROCKY SHORE

*John M. Kingsbury*

*Illustrated by Edward and Marcia Norman*

THE CHATHAM PRESS, INC.
*Old Greenwich, Connecticut*

DISTRIBUTED BY THE VIKING PRESS, INC.

*This book is dedicated to*
WILLIAM H. WESTON, JR.
one of Harvard's great teachers

*Acknowledgments*
The author acknowledges with grateful appreciation the help of several
colleagues including John M. Anderson, H. P. Banks, and Arthur L. Bloom.

TEXT COPYRIGHT © 1970 BY JOHN M. KINGSBURY
ILLUSTRATIONS COPYRIGHT © 1970 BY EDWARD AND MARCIA NORMAN

FIRST PRINTING

LIBRARY OF CONGRESS CATALOG CARD NO.: 71-122758
SBN 85699-015-9

MANUFACTURED IN THE UNITED STATES OF AMERICA
BY THE HALLIDAY LITHOGRAPH CORPORATION.

# Contents

SEASIDE GOLDENROD
*Solidago sempervirens*

*The breaking waves dashed high*
*On a stern and rockbound coast,*
*And the woods against a stormy sky*
*Their giant branches tossed.*

# Introduction

THE granite coast of Maine, the wet elemental fury of a "three day Nor'easter," the conquering grit of a small band of Pilgrims—these are the images evoked by the words of Felicia Dorothea Hemans' *Pilgrims Hymn*. The granite coast of Maine offers to man and to other organisms the beneficence of adversity. Beneficence of adversity seems at first a contradiction in terms, but is not really so, as a closer look at the rocky shore shows. For in this phrase is summed much of significance concerning the life of those organisms: plant, animal, and man, who populate the granite coast and make a sometimes rich, sometimes precarious living from this most unusual of habitats, the shifting interface between land, sea, and air.

Seashores are the edges of the great ocean basins. They have much in common throughout the world—elements such as the saltiness of the seawater, the boundary between liquid and solid, and nearly always, the ocean tides. Yet, the rockbound New England coast is unique in many of its characteristics. The individuality of a particular shore can be traced to two major interacting influences: its geological history and the "mix" of organisms which populate it. This book is about these two things.

In the following pages we present in illustration and in word a description of the rocky New England seashore, designed to provide the reader with a knowledge of the major types of habitats it encompasses, a means of recognizing the principal organisms, both plant and animal, which populate these habitats, and an awareness of how all these things are subtly interrelated and interacting. Here is the real beginning point for those who would apply themselves intelligently to a perceptive appreciation of this complex natural phenomenon—the sea and its boundary—or who would concern themselves with the unhappy results of man's increasing presence next to it and unenlightened exploitation of it.

Much of what is presented here has come from personal experience of the author and illustrators at two of the region's most appropriate locations, Acadia National Park on Mount Desert Island and the Isles of Shoals, offshore at the Maine-New Hampshire state line. Both areas are protected from too great an exposure to the deleterious effects of man, and the richness of the communities of organisms they support gives a measure of what is possible elsewhere under similar conditions.

WILD ROSE *Rosa rugosa*

# The Forming of a Rocky Shore

THE New England shore is sinking. Here is a vivid example of the result of continued slow submergence of the land in relation to the level of the surrounding water. It is called a "drowned" seacoast. Compare what you see in New England with the coast of states from New Jersey southward where submergence is not taking place. There the shoreline is "mature," characterized by vast expanses of nearly level coastal plain, lengthy sand beaches, off-shore islands, and very shallow water.

At a time some three hundred million years ago, the earth's crust at the eastern edge of North America was unstable. Mountain-building activity took place. The rock crust was heated and humped up into a rugged profile of granite. This was the same instability which resulted in the Appalachian mountains farther south. In time the crust stabilized and became quiescent. Then the rugged early New England mountains were slowly worn down in the inexorable process of erosion. The softer, earlier sedimentary materials, wherever they still existed from before the mountain-building time, were washed and scraped down into the valleys, and even the hard granite itself was slowly chipped and worn away by water, wind, freezing and thawing, sun, rain, and the prying roots of plants. A thickness of material which can literally be measured in miles was worn off the mountain ranges. Their height and ruggedness were reduced in similar degree, and thick sediments of eroded material were deposited in the valleys. The terrain became much flatter.

Then came the glaciers. This was an event of greatest importance in sculpturing the land wherever it occurred. Glaciation began in New England about 100,000 years ago and ended about 10,000 years ago, a mere yesterday in geological terms. The ice came and went several times during this period before it finally retreated to approximately its present boundaries. During its maximum development, it too accumulated to a thickness that could be measured in miles, and its weight was nearly beyond comprehension. It covered even the highest peaks of the old New England mountains and scraped ponderously over and between them. It gathered large and small rocks, some weighing hundreds of tons, in its bottom layers, and with them scoured out the sediments of valleys down to bare rock, and even wore away a lot of the underlying granite in many places. The individual scrape marks of boulders drawn across the granite surface can still be seen wherever the original post-glacial surface has been recently exposed.

Everything the glacier picked up was deposited in the form of sand, gravel, and coarse boulders at the various points where the glacier's edge stopped for a while and melted. During glaciation, the land was higher and the ocean lower than now. The glacier extended well out beyond the present margin of the land. Its outer boundary reached as far as Georges Bank which lies at the edge of the continental shelf and marks the outer limits of the Gulf of Maine.

Farther inland, in the old mountains, the glacier worked at the lines of weakness in the underlying granite, especially those which lay more or less parallel to its southward path. Here, where cracks had developed in the granite, the glacier was able to dig deep valleys into rock as it concentrated its weight and its scouring materials in them. As the glacier melted and released its captured water back into the ocean, the level of the water rose in relation to that of the land. The gravel islands at the edge of the continental shelf were submerged, and water rose in the basin of the Gulf of Maine. It lapped higher and higher along the shore line and penetrated farther and farther inland along the valleys that met the shore.

Today, we see the results of all these events: the rounded granite masses, the shoreline following up and down the irregular valleys, the mountains descending into the sea in files separated by north-south valleys. Offshore, the higher elevations stick up out of the water as islands. The whole coastline appears as though it had been "combed" down into the sea. The Gulf of Maine terminates seaward in the fringe of fishing banks, the former gravel islands, principal among which at this latitude is Georges Bank lying about 600 miles to the southeast of the present shoreline. The edge of the continental shelf lies just beyond Georges Bank. Deep ocean basin lies eastward to the Mid Atlantic Ridge, thence eastward further to the continental shelf of Europe from which the North American continent is believed to have separated at some period in the early history of the earth.

The drowning mountain ranges and the deep valleys between them account for the ruggedness of the Maine coast. For each mile of coastline as the crow flies, the actual shoreline is more than ten miles long. Salt marshes and sand beaches

BAYBERRY
*Myrica pensylvanica*

JUNIPER
*Juniperus communis*

occur in relatively few locations, usually where the water level coincides with a gentle valley bottom or shallow embayment. Marshes are in very delicate balance. They can exist only under two conditions. The rate at which they receive sediment from the land runoff must be great enough to keep them building up as fast as the land sinks, and these materials must be spread out over the whole surface of the marsh so that it remains more or less level. Marshes are more common and more extensive in southern New England where the rate of sinking is slower, and this critical balance is, consequently, somewhat easier to maintain. In northern New England, relatively deep water often comes right up to the shore line. This accounts for the numerous ports along the Maine coast. On sandy, gradually sloped coasts the depth of water is the main limitation to where a port can be located; here adequate protection from ocean storms is the primary consideration.

Several kinds of rock may be found on the New England shoreline, but granite is by far the most common. In contrast to most types of rock which are composed of compressed sediments, granite represents once molten material. It is a mixture of several separate substances which crystallize or solidify at different rates as the granite cools from its molten state. The three principal crystals in granite are quartz, which is glassy in nature and has an uneven surface; feldspar, which is pink or gray, opaque, and breaks with an even cleavage pattern; and hornblende, which consists of smaller particles, black in color. The size of each of these crystals is determined by the time taken for it to collect together while the rock was cooling and solidifying. Granite rock near the margins of the molten mass cooled quickly and its crystalline structure is very fine and even. Granite toward the center of the

**BEARBERRY**
*Arctostaphylos uva-ursi*

molten mass cooled very slowly and the mineral crystals of which it is composed are large, coarse, and distinct.

At a time much later than the solidification of the granite rocks, new volcanic activity took place beneath them. Cracks or fissures opened in the granite, and molten rock welled up in them from below. Today one sees the result as vertical dikes of a dark, very fine grained rock. These basalt or trap dikes characteristically have parallel walls, extend for hundreds of feet, and are often several feet wide. They show up clearly where the surface rock is bare as a band of dark against the light colored granite. At the shoreline, trap dikes wear away more rapidly in the water than does the granite on either side, and small caves are sometimes formed.

Geologically speaking, only a brief time has elapsed since the retreat of the glacier and little sediment has accumulated on the bare granite surfaces. This fact is reflected in life along the coast. Agriculture has never been important here. Instead lumbering, fishing, and ship-building have dominated human occupations throughout the history of this part of the country.

Along the entire New England coast, Mount Desert Island represents the processes described above to the greatest degree. The old mountain peaks are higher here than elsewhere, and the valley sides steeper. Somes Sound, a drowned valley, is nearly fjord-like in its characteristics. The southern ends of the granite masses are apt to be abrupt and cliff-like in locations where the moving glacier "plucked off" large chunks of rock as it went by. The northern slopes, in contrast, are more gently rounded, worn thus as the glacier ground and slid upwards over them. In contrast with the moving sand dunes, beaches, and island passes farther south, the coastal currents here have little material to work with; but in some places beaches may become established by movement of sand, or shoal bars of gravel may collect. At Mount Desert Island the beach at Newport Cove is an example of the former; and at Bar Harbor, a well developed gravel shoal of water-tumbled, rounded stones exists between the mainland and the small off-shore islands.

LOW BUSH BLUEBERRY *Vaccinium angustifolium*

# Above the Tides

SPRUCE *Picea spp.*

ALONG the rugged Maine coast, plants of the mountains often come right down to high tide. Mountain Spruces (*Picea* spp.) and juniper (*Juniperus communis*) are conspicuous near the shore. Grayish tangles of bayberry (*Myrica pensylvanica*) may catch the eye. These woody thickets, waist high or taller, bar the way to a leisurely amble, but reward those who brush against them with their fragrance. In late summer, the white, bumpy berries from which a little bayberry wax can be obtained are clustered along many of the woody branches. Lowbush blueberry (*Vaccinium angustifolium*) and its close relative, the bearberry (*Arctostaphylos uva-ursi*), form similar but lower-growing thickets. Both of these bushy plants produce small, fleshy berries later in the season. Everyone is familiar with blueberries, but the wild lowbush blueberries of northern climates have an intensity of flavor that, for many people, more than compensates for their small size. The evergreen bearberry produces small, attractive red berries. Although tasteless and inedible by human standards, bearberries are eaten readily by wild birds. A real northerner is the black crowberry (*Empetrum nigrum*) which is found from the arctic south to Maine. These dwarf, heath-like, spreading shrubs with tiny rolled leaves favor rocky areas of mountains and coasts, a fact reflected in the scientific

**BLACK CROWBERRY**
*Empetrum nigrum*

name (from the Greek, *petros*, meaning rock). Dense stands of crowberry are the source of great quantities of small black berries which are relished by some of the wild birds.

Ferns are familiar inhabitants of woods or abandoned fields near the shore. Bracken fern *(Pteridium aquilinum)* tends to spread the three main divisions of its frond into a broadly triangular outline. Polypody fern *(Polypodium virginianum)* displays a narrow, elongate frond with the leaflet blades arranged ladder-like but alternately along each side of the frond axis. Both ferns uncoil from "fiddleheads" in spring.

Another woodsy plant is bunchberry *(Cornus canadensis)*. This diminutive herb calls attention to itself by its showy white blossoms followed in late summer or fall by a tight cluster of red berries, borne at the tip of the main stem above a whorl of leaves. Bunchberry, like several of the plants above, tends to carpet appropriate locations to the exclusion of most other plants.

Bright splashes of orange on rocks, tree trunks, or old fence posts near the ocean often resolve themselves on close inspection into the flaky crusts of lichens. The most common lichen of the rocky shore is *Xanthoria,* and its orange trail may be followed right down onto the rocks just above high water.

All of these plants have in common the ability to contend successfully with the adversities of the near-shore. One reward for this ability is the absence of other plants not so fortunately adapted for life at the seashore and relief from competition for space and nutrients. The most important adversities of the shore can be summed in one word: dryness. Wind and salt air both tend to draw moisture from plants, and only those able to resist loss of water from within their cells and tissues will be well adapted to life where the ocean's influence is strong.

Ocean water is about three and one-half per cent salt. This means a gallon of seawater evaporated to dryness would yield about a half cup of dry salt. At the edge of the ocean along an exposed rocky shore, winter storms dash great breakers of seawater against the rocks, and the spray is carried far inland by gale winds. Solid water may be carried 50 feet or more up on the rocks, washing out soil, dislodging roots, sweeping away branches, and deluging everything in a concentrated salt solution.

Where the prevailing wind sweeps inland over a continuous expanse of water it meets no obstacle until it reaches the shore. Here its effects are concentrated against those plants struggling to grow erect. In such places, a phenomenon called "wind pruning" may be evident. Bushes at the edge of the shore feel the full effect of the wind and are greatly stunted. Each succeeding bush or tree landward from the shore is partly protected from the wind by the one in front of it and is able to grow a little taller. The whole effect is as though giant clippers had been used to cut the tops of bushes and trees in a horizontal plane ascending from nothing at the edge of the water to the full height of a tree a few hundred feet inland.

At first glance the vegetation above high water does not look very different from that found farther inland. But as one's eye becomes accustomed to the smaller differences, he begins to notice that the seacoast vegetation has a character all its own. There are fewer species of plants, and those present tend to gather in communities or populations which are subtly different from their associations else-

POLYPODY FERN
*Polypodium virginianum*

where. It has often been said that the colors of flowers at the seacoast tend to be deeper or more intense than on the same plants growing farther from the ocean.

Some of the effects of a nearby ocean are detrimental for many plants, but other effects are beneficial. The great mass of the ocean water heats slowly in spring and cools slowly in fall, its temperature lagging about a month behind the seasons on land. Thus it acts like a large thermostat, keeping air temperatures down in summer and warming the overlying air in winter. Some plants can grow surprisingly far north along the coast because here they are not subjected to the killing extremes of cold found just a few miles inland. While cool spring seasons may retard the development of some species, warm falls often keep roses in bloom into November or later in the yards of shoreside villages.

BRACKEN FERN *Pteridium aquilinum*

# The Spray Zone

OF all types of plant habitats, the rocky shore presents the best example of a phenomenon called zonation. Zonation is the distribution of vegetation into distinguishable horizontal belts or bands on a rising land surface. Usually the boundary between bands is relatively sharp; the timberline on mountains is a familiar example. Zonation at the shore is less familiar but far more striking. Here the bands of vegetation and of some sedentary animals, too, are at most a few feet in vertical width. Between high and low tide marks, two or three or even more separate bands can often be distinguished; and what is more remarkable, the same general types of bands can be found on shores an ocean apart. Scientists have been attracted to a study of zonation because it obviously represents a very sensitive response of communities of organisms to their environment, particularly those aspects of the environment which act in a horizontal fashion. Through the study of the causes of zonation, it should be possible to understand much about the distribution of organisms in places where the patterns are less obvious.

Zonation is best seen at a moderately exposed coastal location where the land slopes steeply downwards deep into the water. The first indication of zonation is often apparent from a distance at the time of a good low tide. The rocks display obvious horizontal bands of color. The uppermost band, between the land vegetation and the seaweeds below, consists simply of bare, light-colored granite where almost nothing grows. Just below this, the spray zone (immediately above the highest level to which the water rises) is usually gray or black. This color is caused by the presence of millions of individuals of certain bluegreen algae, each of which is only a few cells in extent and microscopic in size. Bluegreen algae *(Cyanophyta)* are closely related to bacteria, but their cells are generally larger and densely provided with photosynthetic pigments. These pigments, when extracted, display beautiful shades of green, yellow, blue, or sometimes purple, but the massed effect on the rocks is quite sooty. The commonest member of the bluegreen vegetation in the spray zone is a filamentous or thread-like form called *Calothrix*. The thin film of microscopic plant life which it produces, growing on the bare granite, would be easily overlooked except for its color. By virtue of this color, however, these microscopic plants are enabled to use the moisture and nutrients they extract from the water which sprays over them occasionally, combining these materials with carbon dioxide from the atmosphere by means of photosynthesis in the presence of sunlight, and forming the organic matter which they require for growth and reproduction. This is really living close to the fundamentals.

In some places, a black lichen grows in the spray zone. It looks something like an old, rough tar spot. Its name is *Verrucaria*, and it is truly marine. *Verrucaria* can survive and even benefit from total immersion in seawater. A lichen represents the close association of an alga and a fungus, the cells or filaments of which are intertwined. The cooperative association is remarkable because these two different kinds of lower plants are not at all closely related. The fungus accounts for the general shape of the lichen. The alga contributes its capacity for photosynthesis which the fungus, lacking the necessary pigments, is unable to perform by itself.

The surface of the ocean is rarely quiet. Even when the wind is not blowing and collecting the water into waves, the surface of open water undulates up and down. Long-period waves or swells generated by storms hundreds or thousands of miles away extend outward from the edge of the parent storm system and pass majestically and inexorably onward until they encounter a coast. When they meet the rocky shore, they pile up on the rocks and then roll back down, sometimes covering only a few inches, but often many feet. For this reason, it is difficult and imprecise to talk about the high tide mark or low tide mark as though each were a single level to which the water rises on an open shore.

The spray zone is, loosely, that level above high tide which ocean water regularly reaches by splash or spray. Organisms of the spray zone must be opportunistic regarding those activities for which they require water; for, especially in the upper parts of the spray zone, they cannot count on getting wet every day.

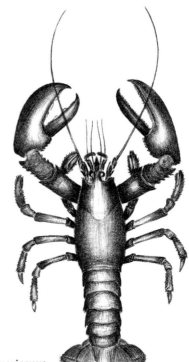

LOBSTER *Homarus americanus*

27

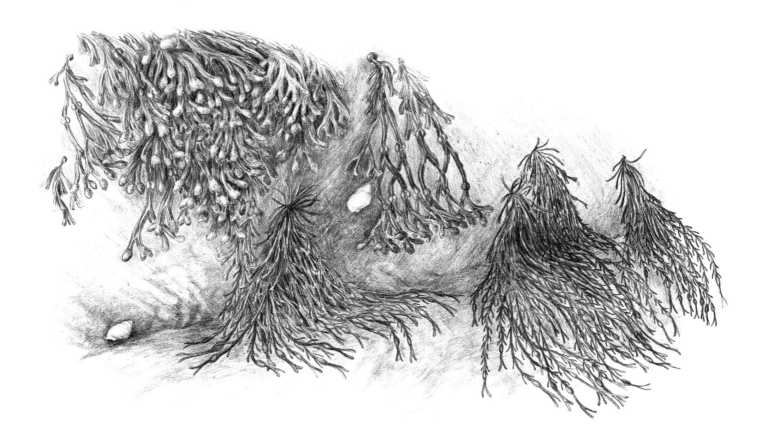

# The Rockweed Zone

THE spray zone merges on its downhill side with the zone next below, that which is regularly and predictably submerged by high tides. At this level we find the first of those plants and animals which require regular wetting, though they can withstand being out of water for extended periods. The most conspicuous of these are the barnacles and periwinkles. Barnacles (*Balanus balanoides*) are light-colored. Periwinkles (*Littorina littorea*) are mostly dark, though there is some variation in shell coloration. Barnacles are fixed to the rock surface, but periwinkles move about freely. The black of the spray zone often extends downward among the barnacles and periwinkles but is soon lost among the seaweeds which make their appearance at this level. Where barnacles are extensive, they create a whitish band beneath the black of the spray zone above.

Periwinkles are snails with shells. They make a living from the vegetation where they occur. Gliding slowly along, they rasp the seaweed surface by means of a small file-like mouth part and eat what they scrape off. Periwinkles are abundant in most places. If you find an active one in shallow water, turn it over and watch the way it gets right side up again. Where they exist in large populations, periwinkles can do a lot of damage to seaweeds; experiments have shown that some seaweeds disappear from an area after a heavy attack. Periwinkles can browse equally well whether they are under or out of water. Certain kinds of periwinkles are very good eating when steamed like clams.

Empty periwinkle shells are often taken over by hermit crabs *(Pagurus longicarpus)*, which usually live below the barnacle zone on the shore. As the crabs grow, they are forced to abandon a shell when they become too big for it and seek a larger one. These crabs, lacking a hard shell of their own, are vulnerable to many enemies when outside the periwinkle shell; so once they have found a new shell, they make the exchange nearly as quickly as one can say it.

Barnacles start life as tiny swimming larvae. At a certain stage of development they settle down, attach themselves firmly to a rock or other solid surface, and secrete the characteristic shell which protects them while they grow to maturity. The shell is very securely cemented to the rock, and the chemical nature of the cement manufactured by barnacles has recently excited the interest of the dental profession. Here is something that really holds, despite alternate drying and wetting.

Barnacles are related to shrimp. They feed on small particles and tiny animals and plants floating in the water. Since they cannot move about and are under water for only a brief period at each high tide, they have to be quick about feeding. When immersed, the shell opens at the top of the cone like a small Vesuvius, and the tiny shrimp-like creature sticks its legs out of the opening. The cluster of long skinny legs looks like a few-toothed, curved comb. They extend slowly, almost straight out, then rapidly curve closed and retract into the shell. This motion is repeated

BARNACLES *Balanus balanoides*
PERIWINKLES *Littorina littorea*

quickly in regular sequence, and particles are thus combed out of the water and brought to the mouth.

The most conspicuous belt of vegetation in the zone between high and low tides is the one next below the barnacles and the bluegreen algae. It is yellow-brown in color and composed of rockweeds. Rockweeds belong to the brown algae. Each plant is coarse and stringy. A closer look shows that there are two main kinds. One is flat in its outer parts with two wings along either side of a somewhat swollen midrib. Where it branches, it often divides into two nearly equal parts. This is the rockweed called *Fucus*. The other is stringy throughout, though each branch is apt to be interrupted by swollen, air-filled bladders at intervals. Some call it the "knotted rockweed." When this plant branches, one branch is usually much smaller than the other, or else branches come out in clusters from the main branch bearing them. This rockweed is *Ascophyllum*.

In the middle part of the zone between high and low tides, one or both types of rockweed will usually be found in abundance. Rockweeds are commonly used to pack lobsters and clams for shipment, and these plants are also used for shore-side clambakes. Unlike higher plants, they do not have stem, leaves or roots which penetrate into soil and take up nutrients. Instead they are anchored to solid rock by a holdfast. If you try to pull one off, the stalk will usually break before the hold-fast comes free. Under water, all parts of the plant have more or less direct access to the nutrients in the seawater bathing them, and all parts have the pigments with which to undertake the process of photosynthesis by which they replenish their tissues and accomplish their other life functions. A way of life in which all parts of

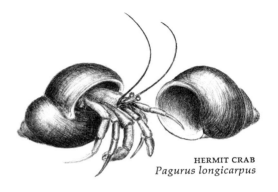

HERMIT CRAB
*Pagurus longicarpus*

the plant can accomplish their own food-making is characteristic of most seaweeds.

Air bladders are found in one kind of *Fucus (Fucus vesiculosus)* as well as in *Ascophyllum*. In the latter they occur in the main axis like knots in a string. In *Fucus*, they occur in the wings, usually in pairs, one on either side of the midrib. The bladders serve to give buoyancy to the branches of the plant, causing them to float nearer the surface when the plant is under water. This is useful in arraying the branches to the best advantage in the light.

Rockweeds reproduce by means of microscopic sexual cells released into the water. These are produced in *Fucus* in the swollen tips which can be found on many of the branches throughout summer. In *Ascophyllum*, the reproductive structures are formed in special short swollen side branches which grow from the main branches in late winter. After they shed their sexual cells in early spring, they quickly become detached from the regular branches, much the way leaves fall from the autumnal tree. Both kinds of rockweeds can live for several years, but die if they are separated from their support. The sexual cells, in starting growth of new plants, begin by attaching to a solid object. Of course, they do not distinguish its size. Some plants start to grow on small stones, mussel shells, or similar supports that later prove inadequate to anchor a fully grown plant. If the support gives way, the plant is lost.

Dog whelks *(Thais lapillus)* look something like large periwinkles, to which they are closely related. Both are spiral, single-shelled molluscs, that have evolved from an elongate ancestor which has lessened its length by twisting up on itself like a turban. Along with the twisting, these animals have lost one of the originally paired sets of bodily organs and have placed the remaining soft viscera up into the shell on top of the head and foot which are found at the mouth of the shell. The head bears two fleshy cone-like tentacles. Periwinkles and whelks move along "at a snail's pace" by means of undulations of the soft, muscular foot. This is best seen by watching an active animal move across a glass plate. All the soft parts can be withdrawn into the shell and the opening closed with a lid-like plate of horny material, the operculum.

Dog whelks vary widely in color and in the smoothness or roughness of their shells. One characteristic helpful in recognizing them is the unusual thickness of the shell and the coarse, heavy lip around its mouth. They reproduce by laying a cluster of small, whitish, vase-like egg cases which are attached to the bottom. Minute shelled whelks issue forth from the cases when they hatch.

Dog whelks unlike their vegetarian cousins, the periwinkles, are meat eaters. They use their rasping apparatus to bore their way through the shells of other animals such as mussels, barnacles, or dead crabs. Thus you often find whelks clustered where there are solid patches of barnacles or young mussels among the rockweeds.

DOG WHELKS AND EGG CASES *Thais lapillus*

# The Irish Moss Zone

AT some point above low tide mark the yellow-brown band of the rockweeds gives way to a diverse population of red seaweeds. Irish moss (*Chondrus crispus*) is frequently the most common of these. It forms dense, often extensive patches of short, stubby, much-branched plants, growing somewhat larger in protected locations or well below low tide mark. In fully exposed, sunny locations, especially near its upper limit, Irish moss is often bleached. Its true color is a deep burgundy red (look for plants growing in the shade of overhanging rockweeds), but bleached plants have yellowish or greenish branches.

The cells of Irish moss yield a very useful jelly or colloid. This wild crop has been harvested for generations at various spots along the northeast coast where it is particularly abundant. In some places it is harvested by men in dories who scrape the underwater rocks laboriously with special long-handled rakes. Elsewhere lobstermen gather Irish moss on beaches after storms bring it ashore. In comparison with these primitive modes of harvest, the extraction, compounding, and uses of the colloid are very sophisticated indeed. It provides bulk in toothpaste, thickening in commercial pies, smoothness in hand creams, non-caloric substance in diet foods, thickening in paint; it stabilizes the chocolate in chocolate milk, the oil in

salad dressings, and sizes a smooth surface on fine papers. Oldtimers still make New England blancmange (a kind of jelled pudding) from the raw plant by heating a few fronds in milk, adding appropriate flavorings, and cooling to a jell in a mold.

Dulse *(Rhodymenia palmata)*, which grows near low tide, looks like a deep red sassafras leaf, or flat plastic glove. Its thick, glistening blades are harvested and dried in some coastal areas, packaged in cellophane bags, or sold in bulk in grocery stores. It can be chewed like chewing gum and has a distinctive "oceanic" flavor which, for most people, takes a little getting used to. The fresh plant can be used the same way. Another common and distinctive red seaweed of the intertidal zone is laver *(Porphyra* spp.). These tissue-like plants come in a number of colors, from light purple to olive-green. Like dulse, the plants grow mostly singly or in small groups, and create spots of differing texture against the background of the other seaweeds where they grow. Laver is not much utilized on our shores, but is an important food material in the Orient. In Japan laver is cultivated by placing poles or ropes on which germlings of the plant have thickly settled into the waters of quiet marine lagoons where the plants grow to full size and are harvested.

If you poke around among the seaweeds between tides, you may be startled by the sudden scuttling of a crab surprised out of its hiding place. It will likely be the rock crab *(Cancer irroratus)* or its close relative, the slightly larger and rougher Jonah crab *(Cancer borealis)*. Both live between tides or below low tide mark. Crabs belong to the crustaceans and, in turn, to the larger assemblage of arthropods. In these two words are summed two of the most important characteristics of crabs: the fact that they bear shells and have jointed appendages. The shells of crustaceans are hornlike in texture and usually are much thinner and lighter than those of molluscs. Instead of the stone-like calcium carbonate of molluscs, crab shells are composed of organic chitin in which some minerals are deposited. The joints in the appendages are areas where the shell remains soft and flexible, enabling the legs, claws, and swimmerets to function effectively. Even though the shell has flexible joints, it does not stretch. As the crab grows, it must periodically replace its old shell with a new, larger one.

Catch a crab and look more closely at it. If you grasp a crab from the rear with your thumb on the top of its shell and your fingers on the bottom, it cannot bring its pincers around to where you are, and you can examine it without risk. A crab is like a lobster folded up. Its tail is curled around underneath and fitted neatly into a flat depression in the abdomen. Crabs are bilaterally symmetrical. Each side bears a large number of appendages which are mirror images of the appendages on the other side. In a general way, the appendages are all similar; but they have been modified in the course of evolution to perform many different functions including sensing, feeding, defending, walking, capturing food, swimming, and for assisting in reproduction. Compare particularly the reduced appendages associated with feeding, which are near the mouth, with the large, claw-bearing legs immediately behind. Watch how a crab uses its legs to walk (if you can find one moving slowly enough). Crabs move smoothly sideways, pulling with the legs on one side while simultaneously pushing with the legs on the other side. Each leg appears to act by itself without regard to what the others are doing.

Crabs are scavengers. They constantly work the shoreline in search of dead,

LAVER
*Porphyra spp.*

37

CORALLINA
*Corallina officinalis*

injured, or defenseless animals which they can catch and devour. They cannot do this with impunity, however, for gulls like nothing better than to catch a crab out in the open; and crabs frequently fight among themselves when they come together. For some reason, the fighting of crabs strikes human beings as comic and fun to watch. Fights in the open usually end in a draw.

Large black areas in the intertidal zone often turn out to be massed populations of the common dark blue mussel *(Mytilus edulis)*. These sedentary animals "seed down" in great quantities from the early swimming stages of the life cycle. They attach themselves firmly to the rock or to other mussels and begin to grow. The attachment consists of a web of fine, but very strong threads, known as the byssus, secreted by each mussel. Mussels are molluscs like the periwinkles and whelks but belong to a different group, the bivalves, the members of which possess two shells instead of one. Their way of life is different, too. Like a barnacle, a mussel can feed only when under water. It opens slightly and creates a current of water between the two shells. This water, carrying microscopic particles of food matter, passes over a surface which is covered with microscopic hairs (cilia). The activity of these cilia serves to capture food particles of the appropriate size from the water stream as it passes.

Another diminutive, but distinctive, inhabitant of the intertidal zone is a whitish-purple, branching plant which might at first be mistaken for a coral. Corallina *(Corallina officinalis)*, a member of the red seaweeds, is most commonly found near the lower limits of the intertidal zone and below. It is one of very few plants able to precipitate lime (calcium and magnesium carbonates) from cold oceanic water. The lime is laid down among the tissues of the plant, "frosting" its tiny fan-shaped segments. Each segment is separated from the ones above and below by a joint where lime is not deposited. The presence of these joints gives the plant some flexibility and allows it to bend with the waves. It can thus successfully inhabit turbulent areas without being seriously broken in the waves. When plants die, the lime remains for a long time after the other tissues have disappeared. Dead plants of *Corallina* are chalk white. True corals (animals) are rare in waters as cold as those found north of Cape Cod.

COMMON MUSSEL *Mytilus edulis*

# The Kelp Zone

**KELP**
*Laminaria saccharina*

THE fourth distinct belt of vegetation that can usually be distinguished on the rocky shore is right at and below the low water mark. The presence of kelps, characteristically large and leathery brown seaweeds, makes this zone conspicuous. On most moderately exposed rocky shores three different kinds of kelp can be found with a little looking. All three are brown to black-brown, several feet long (when mature), and are firmly anchored to a solid bottom by means of a distinctive holdfast. The holdfast consists of a cluster of root-like branches which radiate outward from the single central stalk like a multiple, crooked-finger hand. The three kelps can be told apart by the branching pattern of the blade-like part. *Laminaria saccharina* has a single elongate blade. In summer it has ruffled edges; in winter the edges are not different from the rest of the blade. It looks like a giant razor strop. *Laminaria digitata* is similar except that the blade is wider and divided lengthwise into a half dozen or more individual strops. The third common kelp is *Alaria esculenta* (none of these have recognized common names). The main blade of *Alaria* is long and narrow and has a distinct, sharply defined central midrib down its length. The blade is frayed and torn down to the midrib repeatedly at its outer end. During much of the summer two clusters of smaller, thicker blades arise

**KELP**
*Agarum cribrosum*

from the edges of the stalk between the holdfast and the main blade. These blades are specialized for reproduction and eventually release millions of tiny, swimming cells each of which can result in one or more new *Alaria* plants if everything goes well.

Two other kelps less commonly seen are *Laminaria longicruris* and *Agarum cribrosum*. The first looks much like the simple-bladed *Laminaria saccharina* except that the upper portion of the stalk is gently swollen and hollow. *Agarum* has a blade which is peppered throughout (except at the midrib) with small holes. It is called "devil's apron" by some and the holes represent the effects of sparks in the devil's abode.

How can something as large as a kelp which can weigh up to 25 pounds manage to exist where tumultuous breakers pound against the rocks to which it is attached? A dory or even a lobster pot tied in the same place would be smashed to bits in no time. Kelps live several years, so when you look at a kelp in summer, think of the same place during a midwinter storm, with five- or ten-foot breakers smashing onto and then sucking back from the unyielding granite. Strength with flexibility is the answer. Unlike the rigid dory or lobster pot, a kelp gives with the waves, arching, straightening out, even snapping like a whip in conformity with the water as it rushes past, but not breaking. One measure of the pull required to break a kelp stalk showed about 650 pounds per square inch. It takes even more than this to cause a holdfast to pull free from whatever it is on. Many of the kelps which wash in after a storm bring with them the mussels or stones to which they were attached. Failure of the anchor, not of the plant, caused their death.

The starfish is perhaps the best trademark of the seashore. Different kinds of stars are found along most of the coasts of the oceans. At the rocky New England shore, the common starfish (*Asterias vulgaris*) is five-armed, conspicuously orange-purple (but very variable) and inhabits the zone at low tide and below. Here also are found two near relatives, the brittle star (*Ophiopholis aculeata*) and the sea urchin (*Strongylocentrotus dröbachiensis*). All three are radial animals with a stony outer covering. The tiny calcareous plates of which the covering is made have flexible connections in the common and brittle stars, but form a firm shell in the sea urchin. The common star and sea urchin move about, sometimes quite rapidly, by means of hundreds of tube feet which extend between the bumps or spines. Tube feet wave actively until they contact something, then a sucker-like disc at the tip attaches to it and anchors the foot until it is ready to take another "step." If you can find a starfish about the size of a quarter and if you can get it to attach to your finger and "walk" around it, you will be able to see well how the tube feet work and how flexible the animal is when alive. The tube feet are operated by a single hydraulic system which connects all of them within the animal's body.

**COMMON STARFISH**
*Asterias vulgaris*

Sea urchins also move about by means of tube feet, sufficiently extensible to project beyond the tips of the long spines, but the animals are generally much less active than their starfish cousins. Instead, urchins prefer to hide in rock crevices or to camouflage themselves if out in the open. They do this by placing scraps of seaweeds, bits of shells, or other debris on their backs. Examine a live sea urchin closely. It will perhaps surprise you to see that some of the shorter spines are tipped with small, three-part pincers. Sea urchin spines fit onto the shell by means

**SEA URCHIN**
*Strongylocentrotus dröbachiensis*

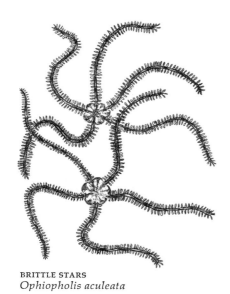

**BRITTLE STARS**
*Ophiopholis aculeata*

of a ball-and-socket joint at the base, attached only by muscles and the skin which covers them (which is why they are readily lost when the animal dies). The pincer spines and tube feet are used in placing camouflage up on top. The common star has similar pincer spines but much smaller. A sea urchin, in fact, is little more than a starfish which has had its arms folded upward and fused together. The shell of a dead sea urchin shows ten double rows of spine-bases running from the anus at the top to the larger opening where the soft mouth parts are on the underside.

However, common stars and sea urchins are quite dissimilar in their feeding habits. The star is a voracious predator, taking in almost any available animal material it comes across in its straight-line journeys. Bivalves such as clams, oysters, and mussels are their favorite food. When a star encounters a clam, for example, it encloses it in an embrace of death by folding its arms around the clam like a fist, with its mouth centered over the edge where the two clam shells come together. The clam, of course, closes up tight. Then there is a tug of war. The star eventually wins if nothing disturbs it, and the clam finally relaxes its large, shell-closing muscle and begins to gap open. Then a curious thing happens. As soon as there is even a little space between the shells, the starfish protrudes its stomach through its mouth, down between the shells into the middle of the clam and proceeds to digest the latter right in place. In contrast, sea urchins are mainly vegetarians, though they too will feed on animal material, but not as aggressively as the star because they do not have the means to open a live shell.

Brittle stars are small, fragile, and very active. They move by means of their long and flexible arms, not by tube feet. The arms are quite distinct from the main body and are easily detached. This is a defense mechanism which allows the animal to escape anything which catches it by an arm or two; it simply leaves them behind. You will find this out if you try to pick one up by the arm. Even if all the arms are lost, the animal is not harmed; it grows new ones. The common star also has great powers of regeneration, and you will often find individuals with an arm either missing or much smaller than the others as a new one regenerates.

Sea cucumbers (*Cucumaria frondosa*) are closely related to starfish, but they certainly do not look it. When relaxed, they look something like a cucumber and may be a foot or more in length. They do not have a hard exterior. Instead, their surface is leathery and muscular, and they can elongate, contract, or contort themselves remarkably. A sea cucumber is like a naked sea urchin pulled out so that the mouth is at one end. The mouth is surrounded by a crown of ten greatly branched tentacles which can be retracted. The body, dark purple on one side, lighter on the other, bears rows of small tube feet. Like its starfish cousins, the sea cucumber has remarkable powers of regeneration. When attacked, it often contorts itself so vigorously that it literally rips itself open, throwing out its viscera in the process. If this stratagem succeeds in defeating the attacker, the cucumber heals, regenerates its missing parts, and returns to normal.

Sea cucumbers live in tide pools or among the rocks near and below the low tide mark where they survive by taking in small particles of organic debris from the water, sand, or mud by means of the moplike branched tentacles around the mouth.

If you are lucky, some day you may find a small mottled green lobster (*Homa-*

*Alaria esculenta*

**KELP**
*Laminaria longicruris*

*rus americanus*) hiding among the rocks at low tide mark, but the place where most persons see lobsters is in a lobster pound or on the table. Lobsters are built like unfolded crabs, with similar appendages, but with tails larger in proportion to the rest of the body. They move on and offshore with the seasons, causing the lobstermen to move their thickets of lobster pot buoys along the coast from time to time. Lobsters are caught in pots whose construction has been closely adapted by trial and error over many generations of human experience to the particular habits of the animals. Depending on who is talking, pots are divided into "kitchen" and "parlor" or "bedroom." They are baited with trash fish, cod heads, or similar fish products, often well-ripened to attract the scavenger appetites of lobsters. That these techniques are successful is shown by the fact that in many areas nearly every lobster is caught within a year of the time it reaches legal size. Since the lobsterman probably catches and releases each lobster several times during the years before it reaches legal size, he can perhaps claim that he is truly farming the sea by repeatedly giving good square meals to immature lobsters. Lobsters are limited in supply and usually bring a good price. But considering the fact that the average lobsterman has several thousand dollars tied up in pots and buoys which he can lose overnight in a bad storm, lobstering is a risky business. A good living can be made lobstering when conditions are favorable, but no genuine Maine lobsterman will admit publicly that things are going well.

In a lobster pound, the crustacean inhabitants are given to fighting with one another. Their claws are immobilized with wooden pegs or rubber bands to prevent their injuring each other and to make them easier to handle. An unpegged lobster can be handled safely the same way as a crab; but if it gets a good grip on a finger with its claw, it can do real damage. Lobster claws differ. On each lobster the biting surface of one claw bears large, white, rounded humps like the cusps on a molar. This claw crushes. The other claw has much sharper points, like incisors which can be used to cut and tear. In some lobsters, one claw is obviously smaller than the other. This results from the loss of the original full-sized claw and its replacement with a regenerating one. When an appendage arm is lost, a special mechanism quickly seals off the opening and prevents the lobster from bleeding to death. Since the shell is inelastic, a new appendage cannot grow forth immediately. Instead it begins to develop within the old shell and appears, somewhat reduced in size, as a new appendage when the animal molts. In molting, a new and very soft shell forms all around the lobster's body, even over the surface of its eyes, within the old shell. The lobster crawls off to hide. Then the old shell splits open at the back of the carapace (between the "back" and the "tail"), and the lobster pulls both its front and tail ends out, freeing itself from the old shell completely. As soon as it is free, it increases in size, the soft new shell stretching as necessary. Then the new shell hardens and the rearmored lobster can come out of hiding.

SEA CUCUMBER *Cucumaria frondosa*

*Laminaria digitata*

# Tide Pools

TIDE pools are places among the rocks between high and low tide marks where seawater is trapped each time the tide goes out. They are very unusual habitats. Plants and animals which populate them never have to withstand drying, and the plants get more light per day than they would below the low tide mark. These are advantages. On the other hand, tide pool water warms readily on a sunny summer day, may be rapidly diluted with freshwater during a thundershower, or may experience quick and marked chemical changes as the result of the accelerated life processes of the plants and animals living in this trapped and briefly stagnant water. Tide pools are therefore more dynamic than the ocean water around them. Most if not all tide pool organisms live elsewhere as well, but some are particularly adapted to the changing water of a tide pool and are characteristic of such locations. A small, shallow pool is fascinating to study on a bright summer day when the sunlight penetrates through the water making everything crystal clear right to the bottom. The longer you look the more you will see as the smaller organisms begin to sort themselves out in your mind. Here are some you will surely see in one tide pool if not another.

The crumb-of-bread sponge (*Halichondria panicea*) takes that name from its

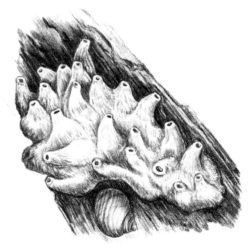

**CRUMB-OF-BREAD SPONGE**
*Halichondria panicea*

somewhat fanciful resemblance to a large piece of broken bread—the old-fashioned kind that broke into coarse fragments. If your mental image of a sponge is the man-made cellulose type, or even the older natural bath sponges from Florida, you will have to change it considerably to accommodate the common New England sponges. A natural bath sponge is merely the cleaned skeleton of the animal which used to live there. The crumb-of-bread sponge has a much less elaborate type of skeleton than the bath sponge, and what you see in a tide pool is the living animal. It encrusts rocks or pebbles with a thick, coarse, irregularly bumpy layer of yellowish or greenish-yellow material of which its substance is composed. In places you can see that it is organized into little chimney-like tubes each with a hole at the tip. Sponges are hardly more than organized colonies of millions of individual, nearly self-sufficient cells. Acting together, they cause water to pass in a slow current through very tiny holes all over the surface into the hollow interior and exit through the large pore at the tip of the "chimney." Small particles of food are trapped from the water as it passes.

Another common tide pool inhabitant is the sea anemone, of which there are several common species. An opened-out anemone is very distinctive with its circle of feathery, tubular tentacles surrounding a central mouth. The fancied resemblance of this to a flower accounts for the common name of this group of sedentary animals. Anemones are attached firmly to the solid bottom and if you try to remove one you will only injure it. They look as though they were firmly and permanently affixed, but anemones do move slowly from place to place by means of a gliding motion of the solid "foot" of the animal. Anemones live by capturing food organ-

SEA ANEMONE
*Metridium senile*

isms from the water. When a small fish brushes against a tentacle, all the tentacles in that spot will abruptly curl in on it and catch it. The food is then passed to the mouth, as many tentacles cooperating as necessary.

If you disturb an anemone, you will find that the defense mechanism of these shell-less animals is to retract all of the tentacles suddenly and to contract in on itself until the original barrel-shaped individual becomes a small gelatin-like blob. It does this by means of two sets of muscles, one encircling it and the other running lengthwise of the body. Another defense mechanism which may also help in food gathering are the tiny, worm-like threads which can be discharged by the animal. These bear microscopic stinging cells. Though not troublesome to man's thick skin, the stinging cells can inject a paralyzing substance into small animals. Anemones reproduce sexually and also by simple budding. In budding, a piece of the old animal merely separates itself and makes a new one. Anemones have only one opening for the digestive tract, so what is not digested is eventually eliminated back out the mouth. Most tide pool anemones are relatively small—an inch or two tall when expanded. The common larger anemone (*Metridium senile*), however, can become six or eight inches tall and six inches or more across under favorable circumstances.

Limpets (*Acmaea testudinalis*) and chitons (*Chaetopleura apiculata*) are common in tide pools, attached to rocks or shells. Both are snails (single-shelled molluscs as opposed to bivalves) and look much like each other, but one is primitive and the other quite advanced. The chiton is the primitive one. Its flat, oval shell is divided into eight plates, and its body displays full bilateral symmetry of internal organs. Limpet shells are not divided into separate pieces; and although the shell

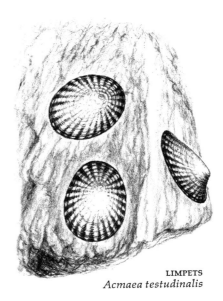

**LIMPETS**
*Acmaea testudinalis*

is nearly symmetrical when viewed from above, the animal itself has only one of the original two sets of bodily parts in its viscera, thereby displaying its relationship to periwinkles, whelks, and other snails. Both chitons and limpets possess rasping mouthparts and make a living by scraping microscopic vegetation and organic matter off the surface of the rocks and shells as they move slowly across them. When a chiton is actively moving, it is only lightly attached to the surface under it. If you try to pick it up, it will immediately attach itself with a firmness that is surprising. To collect a chiton, one must remove it quickly by slipping a knife blade beneath it before it has time to react. When a chiton is removed from seawater, it tends to roll up tightly by bending the flexible joints between the parts of the shell. Because of its appearance while in this position, it is sometimes called armadillo snail.

Many green seaweeds flourish in tide pools, while red and brown seaweeds, which tend to be more sensitive to the factors that make tide pools different from the rest of the intertidal shore, are uncommon or absent. Some green seaweeds form cloudy masses of thin green threads in the water. Others such as *Spongomorpha* are composed of rather coarse threads tangled together into distinctive tufts or ropes attached somewhere to solid bottom. Still others are formed as cellular sheets or tubes. *Enteromorpha intestinalis* is an example of the latter. It forms a long, usually unbranched tube, which may become as much as a half inch in diameter and a foot or more in length. Most other species of this plant are smaller, some even thread-like and branched, yet all are tubular and hollow throughout. The hollow cavity of *Enteromorpha intestinalis* traps the gases (principally oxygen)

*Enteromorpha intestinalis*

manufactured by the plant during photosynthesis, and on a warm, sunny day the tubes become filled with large gas bubbles which float them to the surface of the tide pool where, as the name suggests, they look like a mass of tangled, bright green intestines.

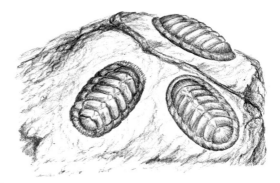

CHITONS *Chaetopleura apiculata*

# The Sandy Beach

SANDY beaches, though far less common in northern New England than farther south, occur in some pockets of shore north of Boston. Sand is an unusual environment and has attracted a number of kinds of organisms which have evolved specializations to exploit it. The companion volume to this book, *The Sandy Shore* by John Hay, discusses common plants and animals of the sand beaches and mud flats around Cape Cod. They do not differ greatly from those of the colder beaches and mud flats farther north.

Among the higher plants populating the sand strand above extreme high tide mark will commonly be found the wild rose (*Rosa rugosa*) with floppy, faded-red or white petals and enormous bright red hips (fruits) in late summer; the beach pea (*Lathyrus japonicus*), whose leaves end in tendrils and whose leaflets fold together in bright sunlight; and the low-growing yellow-flowered hudsonia or beach heather (*Hudsonia ericoides*). Scattered plants or stands of orache (*Atriplex patula*), an herb with distinctive arrowhead leaves, or sea rocket (*Cakile edentula*), a much branched annual mustard with fleshy leaves and purple to pink to white flowers may be encountered. Another inhabitant of the sand is seaside goldenrod (*Solidago sempervirens*) with thicker leaves and somewhat showier flowers than its more familiar inland counterpart.

ORACH
*Atriplex patula*

BEACH HEATHER
*Hudsonia ericoides*

A sandy beach is a good place to examine the jetsam cast up by the retreating tide. Most of the seaweeds and animals that inhabit the waters below low tide and can otherwise be obtained only by diving or dredging, end up on the shore sooner or later, especially after a storm. Shells persist for a long time, of course, and can be studied at leisure, but much of the rest of the cast-up plant and animal life will soon decay beyond recognition. Look for the freshest, which is to say the most recent, windrow left by the latest high tide as it changed. Ignore orange peels, watermelon rinds, aluminum beer cans, upside down pop bottles, and immortal plastic debris which come ashore indiscriminately from small and large vessels passing by, and resolve not to toss things overboard when you go out on the ocean.

Tufts or tangles of delicate red seaweeds, sometimes free, sometimes attached to other coarser seaweeds, are very common in the cast drift. One of the many types is *Ceramium,* which on close examination with a sharp eye, or even better with a magnifying lens, displays bands of lighter and darker color across the branches, like zebra stripes. When actively growing, the branch tips end in little pincers that look like lobster claws. If you had trouble finding kelps at low tide, look again for them in the wash. Especially interesting are the holdfasts, for they support a variety of other organisms, both plant and animal. One of the most delicate and beautiful of red seaweeds is the diminutive *Euthora,* with its striking deep red color and lacy branching pattern. Since it grows only below low tide, the best place to look for it is in the drift line.

Among the common shells are those of mussels and sea urchins described earlier. Also present in the drift should be the shells of the common or waved whelk

(*Buccinum undatum*), the ten-ridged neptune (*Neptunia decemcostata*) and, occasionally, sand dollars (*Echinarachnius parma*). The sand dollar is the shell of a close relative of the sea urchin and is built on the same general pattern. In the living animals the spines are tiny and thickly crowded on the surface so that it looks almost like fur. They are soon lost after the animal dies, because like the larger spines of the sea urchin, they are attached to the skeleton only by the thin layer of skin and muscle which covers them when alive. Ten-ridged neptunes and the waved whelk are snails, related in structure and feeding habits to the periwinkles, dog whelks, and limpets described earlier. These two are somewhat larger, but are still relatively small compared with some of the other whelks, such as the channeled whelk (*Busycon carica*) which is common in southern New England. Ten-ridged neptunes and the waved whelks are sharply pointed at the tip of the spiral. The ten-ridged neptune takes its name from the presence of spiral thickenings down the shell which look like screw threads. The waved whelk, in contrast, has indistinctly defined bands or waves running lengthwise of the shell, across the spirals.

BEACH PEA
*Lathyrus japonicus*

COMMON OR WAVED WHELK *Buccinum undatum*

# Salt Marshes and Mud Flats

COMPARED with the rocky shore, which has some geological longevity, the salt marsh is a tender and transitory event. As the New England coast subsides, marshes can exist only in those protected locations where sediment can spread out evenly and where the rate of addition of sediment can keep up with the rate of sinking of the land. The organisms of the salt marsh are in particularly dynamic relationship with one another and with the environment, for the colonization of an area by any one organism almost always profoundly affects the ability of other organisms to live there successfully.

Typical New England salt marshes consist of nearly pure stands of salt marsh grass (*Spartina alterniflora*, the tall one, and *S. patens*, the short one). These form nearly level expanses of vegetation just above high tide line. Tall salt grass grows nearer water, such as along the marsh shore or the creeks, while short salt grass is limited to somewhat higher land. Short salt grass tends to fall into flattened, swirling mats, easily seen from a distance. You are not as likely to get your feet wet in this kind of marsh as in those where the tall salt grass grows. Salt grasses bind the sediment and form a thick sod. At the same time, these plants can keep "climbing" on top as new sediment is added to the marsh. Salt marsh hay, which was once

SEASIDE PLANTAIN
*Plantago juncoides*

59

TUBEWORM *spirorbis*
ON *Fucus vesiculosus v. spiralis*

fed to livestock, has found use more recently as a garden mulch. It has the advantage over other types of straw mulch because salt hay seed will not germinate and grow in ordinary soil, and it is usually free of weed seeds.

Occasional plants of other vegetation begin to appear in the salt marsh with increasing frequency toward its landward edge. One of these is seaside plantain *(Plantago juncoides)*, a low-growing herb, grass-like in general appearance but with thicker, fleshier leaves. Presence of this plant is an indication that the salt content of the marsh soil is reduced.

If the salt marsh descends gently to the edge of open water, it will usually terminate in a more or less extensive mud flat. The mud flat goes under water at high tide and salt grass is unable to populate it. Instead, resistant or depauperate seaweeds make up the principal vegetation if any is found at all. Some rockweeds, washed into a mud flat, anchor and establish themselves, continuing to grow vegetatively, though they lose powers of sexual reproduction under such circumstances. Their general appearance under these unusual conditions changes markedly, and they receive recognition as special varieties by the botanist. One such is *Fucus vesiculosus* variety *spiralis*. The fronds of the open ocean plant are more or less flat. In the mud flat variety, they are conspicuously and regularly twisted in a spiral. Tiny white coils are often scattered on the surface of the fronds. On closer inspection these turn out to be little limey tubes, the homes of a small marine worm *(Spirorbis* spp.).

The salt marsh and mud flats are very rich areas. Much of the life which makes them so is inconspicuous, buried, or microscopic and, therefore, easily overlooked.

Yet these lands and their interrelated workings are critical to the life of many organisms, some of which spend only a short but absolutely necessary part of their life cycle here. Salt marshes need protection. They are in very delicate balance even without the influence of man. Without them we would lose certain plants and animals, some which are important to man now and others which might become so.

Important burrowing animals in the mud flats or on gentle sandy beaches near and below low tide include clams and quahogs (more familiar to most people on the table). Both are bivalve molluscs which burrow down into the mud, leaving a small tunnel to the surface through which they pass a current of water. They feed on small food particles in the water the same way a mussel does as described earlier. Quahogs (*Mercenaria mercenaria*) have thick shells, usually rough on the outer surface and marked with blue or purple, especially on the smooth inner surface. Small quahogs are called cherrystones. The soft shelled clam (*Mya arenaria*) has a very delicate shell which a strong person can squash between his fingers. Gulls eat either kind voraciously and are quite adept at getting past the quahog's heavy shell. They repeatedly take a quahog six feet or more into the air and drop it on a hard surface such as a large stone or a roadway until the quahog shell breaks open. Gulls habitually use certain rocks or particular spots in roadways, which can be recognized by the accumulation of empty or broken shells around them.

Two other molluscs of the mud flats are the razor clam, a bivalve; and the common whelk (*Buccinum undatum*), a snail described above. The razor clam (*Ensis directus*) is extremely capable at burrowing, and its elongate shape helps. When disturbed, it burrows rapidly, straight down in mud. Starting prone on the

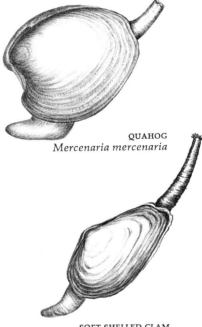

QUAHOG
*Mercenaria mercenaria*

SOFT SHELLED CLAM
*Mya arenaria*

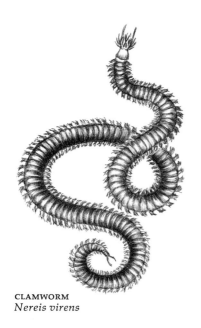

**CLAMWORM**
*Nereis virens*

surface of a mud flat, a razor clam first upends itself before it starts to dig itself down into the mud by means of a muscular foot which it projects from one end of the shell and buries in the mud. Then the tip of the foot swells, serving as an anchor, while the rest of the foot contracts. The contraction causes the tip of the shell to be pulled down into the mud, and acting like a stick pulled into a hole end first, the rest of the shell rears up. The foot then repeats its digging, swelling, and contracting; and with each repetition, the shell moves an inch or so farther into the mud until soon it has entirely disappeared.

Clams and quahogs are commercially important. So are the clam worm *(Nereis virens)*, blood worm *(Glycera* sp.), and lugworm *(Arenicola marina)* which are in demand as fishing bait. Clam worms live in burrows in mud or muddy sand, remaining quiescent during the day but coming out to feed on crustaceans and other small animals at night. They are closely related to earthworms which they resemble in general shape and size. They differ from earthworms most conspicuously in their two rows of appendages, one down either side. Earthworms have very thin appendages, while those of clam worms are large, complex and serve for swimming and burrowing or creeping. Clam worms possess an iridescent sheen, and their grace of motion when swimming is something you will remember if you have the good fortune to see it.

**RAZOR CLAM** *Ensis directus*

# The Open Sea

THE sea itself is populated by thousands of kinds of plants and animals from the microscopic to the gigantic. The pasturage of the sea is composed of microscopic plants. These serve as the starting point of a chain of bigger-eats-smaller to an end point which is often harvested by man. Here are just a few of the interesting marine animals from the open ocean and continental shelf.

Two important commercial fishes from the Gulf of Maine are the haddock (*Melanogrammus aeglefinus*) and the cod (*Gadus callarias*). Both are members of the cod family of fishes, and both are bottom and near-bottom scavengers eating nearly everything they come across. Cod can grow as large as 70 pounds and in some seasons are the main crop of the small New England trawler or gill-netter. Each codfish has a spot of boneless muscle about the size of a large sea scallop in each cheek and another in the floor of the mouth. These are called "cheeks and tongues" by the fishermen and are considered the best eating parts of the fish. Mostly, however, they are thrown away with the head when the cod is cleaned and packed in ice on board ship because there is no market to pay for the extra trouble of cutting them out.

Although these fishes are desired by the fishermen, the dogfish is his enemy.

The dogfish (*Squalus acanthias*) is a small shark and, therefore, a member of the non-bony, primitive fishes. They school in the thousands or millions off the New England coast at certain times of year during their annual migrations. Dogfish and larger sharks are vicious predators, chasing fish, ripping them apart, and devouring them in a frenzy of excitement. Dogfish not only have no commercial value in themselves but also can cause a lot of trouble to nets and catch.

The Atlantic blackfish (*Globicephalus* sp.) is not a fish at all; it is a small whale, and whales are marine mammals, giving birth to live young and suckling them after birth. Another marine mammal, one seen more often from a shore location, is the northern harbor seal (*Phoca vitulina*). These marine mammals have gone back into the sea from an earlier land ancestry. The seals show their origins best. Their limbs are only partly modified as flippers, and they still spend much of their time out of water basking on rocks, especially on the more remote offshore islands and shoals. Whales and true porpoises are more fully modified for spending their lives in the ocean and are quite fish-like in appearance. Two modifications of interest are the blowhole which serves as a means of getting air to and from the lungs (marine mammals lack gills), and the tail fin which is horizontal instead of vertical as in true fishes. Whales swim by undulating the tail fin up and down instead of from side to side as do fishes. Marine mammals generally possess a high degree of intelligence as shown by their actions and their complex means of communicating audibly with one another. They can be taught to perform complicated tasks and are usually star attractions in marine aquaria.

No discussion of the northern rocky shore would be complete without men-

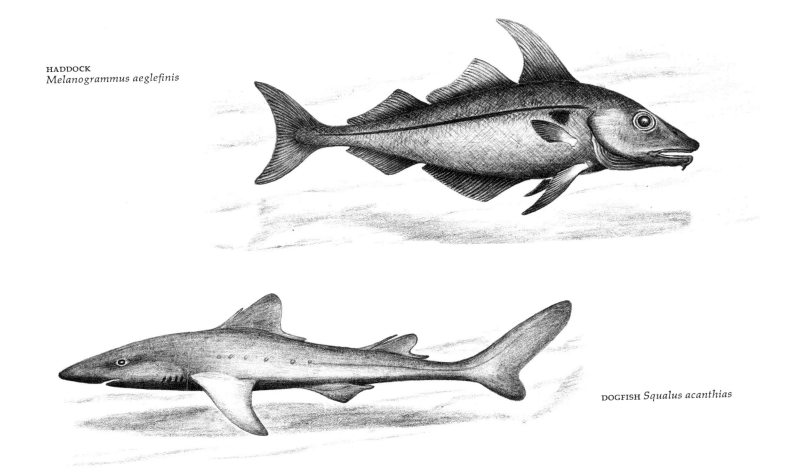

**HADDOCK**
*Melanogrammus aeglefinis*

DOGFISH *Squalus acanthias*

tion of gulls. We have several species, the most conspicuous of which are the herring gull *(Larus argentatus)* and the great black backed gull *(Larus marinus)*. The latter is the largest of gulls, with a wing spread of up to 5 feet, and is called "the minister" by fishermen. Normally, a gull consumes fish, molluscs, or dead animals by the shore and makes an honest living. Man has changed all that. Gulls now find it easier to live from man's garbage dumps. Just as garbage dumps have increased along the coast, so have the gulls. Now the gulls are in the midst of a population explosion and have become not only a nuisance but also a danger, the greatest of which is the accidents they can cause to aircraft which are landing or taking off. Gulls require nesting grounds during the spring and early summer egg-laying season and have taken over many offshore islands for this purpose, driving off the other birds previously there and destroying the vegetation with their concentrated excrement. Right now the black backed gull is increasing at the expense of the herring gull since it is able to dominate in the competition for the most desirable nesting locations.

Long-necked, coal black birds flying over the water are apt to be cormorants *(Phalacrocorax antitus)*, sometimes called shags. These birds are excellent fishermen. They nest on isolated rocky shores and in spring lay several light blue eggs, each about the size of a large hen's egg. The naked or fuzzy young birds are unable to fly for some weeks until they get their adult plumage. During this time they must be fed by the parents. The adults catch fish and return to the nest where they are met by a characteristic head weaving or bobbing display by the young chicks. The parents respond to this by regurgitating the caught fishes into the waiting mouths of the chicks. One parent must always remain by the nest to protect the young from gulls. Cormorants are related to pelicans and have a similar but smaller dull orange, inflatable pouch under the lower bill.

HARBOR SEAL *Phoca vitulina*

CORMORANTS *Phalacrocorax antitus*

# The Beneficence of Adversity

$P$LANTS and animals which live on the rocky shore have to endure the many adverse features of both land and ocean: the drying effect of the salt water and the deluges of fresh rain water; the burning of the summer sun and the scraping of the winter sea ice; the grinding of rocks as they roll about in the incessant swells and the wrenching tug of storm breakers; the alternate drying and wetting by changing tides; and, perhaps most difficult of all, the intense competition for attachment and for food. On the other hand, an organism which adapts to the rigors of the rocky shore enjoys some remarkable benefits such as the leveling of climatic temperature extremes; the rapid removal of waste as water surges past; the distribution of food material in the water mass and its passive transport to sedentary animals. Plants benefit greatly from the increased mineral nutrition from land water runoff and the opportunity for photosynthesis in full light when the tide is out. Above all is the richness of food production. As tangible proof of its beneficence, the shoreline is one of the most productive of all known environments.

A vastly complex and shifting web of living interactions has developed from the cycles of the organisms which produce, consume, and produce again as they interrelate to each other and adapt to their environment. Consequences from any

SEA ROCKET
*Cakile edentula*

single event spread outward into three dimensions of intertidal space and spread forward in time in ways that are neither immediately obvious or entirely free from influence by chance alone. Some of the results are surprises which are heightened by our lack of fundamental knowledge and our propensity to interpret what we find from a land-based, all too anthropocentric point of view.

The balance is always delicate. In many instances the web of interactions can magnify an initial event a thousandfold or more. The increasing concentration of DDT as it is passed upward through the food chain of shoreside organisms shows us that. An event of no significance to a particular organism during one stage of its life cycle may result in its mass mortality at another.

What man does near the shore can have and probably will have consequences far beyond our present power to predict accurately or even guess at. We have just begun to learn what real resources are present in the oceans and along the shores of the world. A recent book summarizes more than 300 active substances now known to be obtainable from marine organisms, and the surface of this subject is hardly scratched. Some of these compounds already serve as useful drugs for man's benefit; many others remain to be exploited; and vastly more undoubtedly will be discovered. It is probable that any major interference by man in the delicate balance of the shore's natural environment will have major consequences for the organisms living there. It is entirely conceivable that some of the innocent acts of man may result in the elimination of one or more species of organisms now contributing to the richness of the web of life at the shore. It is equally conceivable that with the loss of one organism may go the loss of a bit of biochemical activity

*Euthora cristata*

which some day might have been developed into a life-saving drug, or might have given insight into a fundamental biological event such as cancer.

Before you vote to fill or drain a marsh, establish a new dump, allow a community to continue dumping raw sewage, permit a utility to heat millions of gallons of water at the shore or an industry to discharge chemicals into an estuary, consider their effect on this delicate balance. Still better, learn what is going on near your shore and how you can influence it to the benefit of continued environmental integrity and hence to the long-term benefit of man.

TEN-RIDGED NEPTUNE *Neptunea decemcostata*

SAND DOLLAR *Echinarachnius parma*

# Index

Page numbers in italic indicate illustrations.

Cancer
   *borealis, 34, 36*
   *irroratus, 36*
*Ceramium, 56*
*Chaetopleura apiculata, 51, 53*
Chiton, *51–2, 53*
*Chondrus crispus, 34, 35*
Clam
   Quahog, *61, 61*
   Razor, *61–2, 62*
   Soft Shelled, *61, 61*
Clam Worm, *62, 62*
Cod, 65
*Corallina officinalis, 38, 38–9*
Cormorant, *68–9, 69*
*Cornus canadensis, 7, 20*
Crab
   Hermit, *30, 31*
   Jonah, 36
   Rock, 36
Crowberry, Black, *19, 20*
*Cucumaria frondosa, 45, 47*
Cucumber, Sea, *45, 47*
*Cyanophyta, 26*

Dogfish, *65–6, 67*
Dulse, *36, 36*

*Echinarachnius parma, 57, 73*
*Empetrum nigrum, 19, 20*
*Ensis directus, 61, 62*
*Enteromorpha intestinalis, 52, 52*
*Euthora Cristala, 56, 72*

Fern
   Bracken, *20, 22*
   Polypody, *20, 21*
*Fucus*
   *vesiculosus, 32*
      var. *spiralis, 60, 60*

*Gadus callarias, 65*
*Globicephalus* spp., 66
*Glycera* spp., 62
Goldenrod, Seaside, *5, 55*
Grass, Salt Marsh, *59, 60*
Gull
   Great Black Backed, 68
   Herring, *68, 68*

Haddock, *65, 67*
*Halichondria panicea, 49, 49*
Heather, Beach, *55, 56*
*Homarus americanus, 27, 45–6*

*Hudsonia ericoides, 55, 56*

Irish Moss, 35

Juniper, *14, 19*
*Juniperus communis, 14, 19*

Kelp, *41, 41–2, 42, 46*

*Laminaria*
   *digitata, 41, 47*
   *longicruris, 42, 46*
   *saccharina, 41, 41–2*
*Larus*
   *argentatus, 68, 68*
   *marinus, 68*
*Lathyrus japonicus, 55, 57*
Laver, *36, 37*
Lichen
   Black, 26
   Orange, 20
Limpet, *51, 51–2, 57*
*Littorina littorea, 29, 30*
Lobster, *27, 31, 45–7*
Lugworm, 62

*Melanogrammus aeglefinis, 65, 67*

*Mercenaria mercenaria*, 61, 61
*Metridium senile*, 50, 51
Mussel, Common, *34, 38, 44, 56*
*Mya arenaria*, 61, 61
*Myrica pensylvanica*, *13, 19*
*Mytilus edulis*, *34, 38*

Neptune, Ten-ridged, *57, 73*
*Neptunea decemcostata*, *57, 73*
*Nereis virens*, 62, 62

*Ophiopholis aculeata*, *43, 44*
Orach, *55, 55*

*Pagurus longicarpus*, 30, 31
Pea, Beach, *55, 57*
Periwinkle, *29, 30, 30, 33, 38, 52, 57*
*Phalacrocorax antitus*, *68, 69*
*Phoca vitulina*, 66, *69*
*Picea* spp., *19, 19*
*Plantago juncoides*, *59, 60*
Plantain, Seaside, *59, 60*

*Polypodium virginianum*, *20, 21*
*Porphyra* spp., *36, 37*
*Pteridium aquilinum*, 20, 22

Quahog: *see clam*

*Rhodymenia palmata*, *36, 36*
Rocket, Sea, *55, 71*
Rockweed, *31–2, 60*
*Rosa rugosa*, *8, 55*
Rose, Wild, *8, 55*

Sand Dollar, *57, 73*
Seal, Harbor, 66, *69*
Seaweed: *see Algae*
Shag, 68
*Solidago sempervirens*, *5, 55*
*Spartina*
  *alterniflora*, 59
  *patens*, 59
*Spirorbis* spp., 60
Sponge, Crumb-of-bread, *49, 49, 50*

*Spongomorpha*, 52
Spruce, Mountain, *19, 19*
*Squalus acanthias*, 66, *67*
Starfish
  Brittle, *43–4, 44*
  Common, *43, 43–4*
*Strongylocentrotus drobachiensis*, *43, 43*

*Thais lapillus*, *32, 33*
Tubeworm, *60, 60*

Urchin, Sea, *43, 43–5, 56–7*

*Vaccinium angustifolium*, *17, 19*
*Verrucaria*, 26

Whelk
  Channeled, 57
  Common or Waved, *56–7, 57, 61*
  Dog, *32–3, 33, 57*

*Xanthoria*, 20

# RENEWALS 458-4574
## DATE DUE

| | | | |
|---|---|---|---|
| SEP 2 3 2008 | | | |
| | | | |
| | | | |
| | | | |
| | | | |
| | | | |
| | | | |
| | | | |
| | | | |
| | | | |
| | | | |
| | | | |
| | | | |
| | | | |
| | | | |
| | | | |
| | | | |